MEMORY

LACE DESIGNS – A VERSION OF TEXTILE DECORATION FROM 1920–1930

ARRANGED AND EDITED BY WOLFGANG HAGENEY

BELVEDERE

EDITION BELVEDERE CO. LTD., ROME - MILAN (ITALY)

BELVEDERE
PAPERBACK
FASHION
TEXTILES
GRAPHIC
DESIGNS
VOLUME 8

A12939

MEMORY

PUBLISHED BY
EDITION BELVEDERE CO. LTD.
ROME–MILAN (ITALY)

© COPYRIGHT 1981
BY EDITION BELVEDERE

PRINTED IN ITALY BY
STUDIO TIPOGRAFICO, ROME
PHOTOLITHOGRAPHY BY
ART COLOR OFFSET, ROME
PHOTOCOMPOSITION BY
ARTWORK TYPE SHOP, ROME

ISBN 88-7070-010-0
EDITION BELVEDERE CO. LTD 00196 ROME/ITALY, PIAZZALE FLAMINIO 19 - TEL. (06) 360.44.88/360.29.60

From the detailed documents...

When decorative designs and motifs leave a lasting impression on our memory, like a pattern, and a certain feeling, an already familiar perception is awoken in our subconscious on a later visual encounter with them (similar to the sense of smell), then ornaments of memory are – like children's dreams – formed in us.

with their mysterious background material...

Our vocabulary and linguistic capacity are undoubtedly formed not only through our social environment or upbringing, but are rather the outcome of the way in which we develop preferences for particular linguistic formulations and sentence constructions, corresponding to our character and temperament. We derive pleasure from the sound and rhythm of individual words which seem to promise more than their mere meaning would have us believe! We derive a subtle or cryptic fascination from plays on words and combinations of words, because they release unexpected associations, because they enrich our imagination or quicken our inspiration. Our eyes work according to a similar principle. Through them all of us have stored up visual images, or are at least ready to admit them into our mind, because colors and forms are a source of fascination to us and stimulate our fantasy.

an elementary repertoire disloses itself...

The possibilities clash with each other. On the one hand, we allow ourselves to be influenced by everyday things and by our immediate environment, spontaneously placing every conceivable combination in the spotlight of a creative sensibility and achieving thereby promising results. On the other hand, we consult the knowledge and experiences derived from already tested prescriptions, in the hope of discovering, through special montage techniques or sophisticated lighting methods, a different light, an extreme variant, the algebra of hypercreativity.

Yet when it finally emerges that we have not so much developed a new syntax as arranged a new context from set pieces, fragments of ideas or bits of ornament, the question is posed: what is it we continuously fall back on? On decorative models.

furnished with cyphers of the most secret equations...

The symbolic and pictorial language of modern commercial art, as also of international high fashion, is expressed in endless retrospective series of continuously recurring patterns and motifs. These seem to form part of a decorative grammar which conditions cultural history and cannot be done without. We thus find, for example, basic structures of lace which were developed since the 16th century in Italy as independent by–products of textile art, and which are still being re–interpreted and modified today – even if endlessly copied and varied – as form elements or macro–ornaments in advertising or in fashion.

They are consequently used on vanity fair, for they undoubtedly add beauty and charm to the motley world of daily reality: hieroglyphs of longing.

and fundamental possibilities for the alternative...

Immeasurably enlarged or unconventionally utilized structural elements – widely removed from their original context – not infrequently collide with the totality of their original material and develop a virtually conceptual relation by being brought into contact with each other, similar to space–time relationships.

Macro–technology as the guarantee of a new type of ornament, as a catalyst to achieve new graphic qualities from fixed form–ideas, to draw new contours: icons of technology, sand dunes of fantasy.

to the wound image of the creative.

In the quest for the ornaments of memory, of the emigration into our inner being, we encounter, in the galleries and halls of our pictorial and motif–world, the almanac of an inexhaustible design–arsenal, the soft geometry of our imagination: models of a deco–construction kit, anatomies of dream landscapes.

Dai documenti dettagliati...

Se disegni decorativi e motivi lasciano nella nostra memoria un'impressione persistente e nello stesso tempo un modello e se durante un successivo incontro visivo (analogamente a quanto accade per l'olfatto) si determina, come su richiamo, nuovamente una nuova sensazione, una percezione familiare, allora si formano – così come accade per i sogni della fanciullezza – ornamenti del ricordo.

con il loro materiale enigmatico di sfondo...

Il nostro patrimonio e la nostra capacità linguistica non vengono indubbiamente formati soltanto dall'ambiente sociale o dall'educazione, ma noi sviluppiamo, secondo il nostro carattere e il nostro temperamento, una preferenza per determinate strutture linguistiche e per determinati fraseggi. Troviamo piacere al suono e al ritmo di parole bizzarre che sono più promettenti di quanto non possa farci credere il loro semplice significato: ricaviamo da giochi di parole e combinazioni di parole uno stimolo sottile o recondito in quanto essi liberano associazioni inattese, agiscono come ispirazione, agiscono come immaginazione.

Il nostro occhio lavora secondo un principio analogo. Abbiamo memorizzato tutti questi elementi o siamo quanto meno pronti ad accoglierli in noi in quanto i colori e le forme producono fascino e stimolano la nostra fantasia: immagini visive.

si apre uno strumentario elementare...

Le possibilità si incrociano. Da un lato ci lasciamo influenzare da cose ricavate dai ritmi quotidiani e dall'ambiente che ci è vicino, poniamo spontaneamente tutte le possibili combinazioni nel cono di luce di una sensibilità creativa realizzando in tal modo risultati pieni di promesse. D'altra parte ricorriamo al sapere e alle esperienze di ricette già collaudate, con la speranza di scoprire, mediante tecniche speciali di montaggio o raffinati metodi di illuminazione, un'altra luce, una estrema variante, l'algebra di una ipercreatività.

Però quando infine si riscontra che noi abbiamo sviluppato meno una nuova sintassi ma elaborato un nuovo contesto partendo da elementi scenici mobili, frammenti di idee e schegge ornamentali, emerge la domanda a cosa noi ricorriamo permanentemente e costantemente: a esempi decorativi.

provvisto di cifre di equazioni segrete...

Il linguaggio dei segni e delle immagini della moderna grafica d'uso, come pure della "high fashion" internazionale mostra in retrospettiva interminabili serie di modelli e motivi sempre ricorrenti che sembrano essere parte di una grammatica decorativa alla quale appunto non si può rinunciare per motivi connessi con la storia della cultura.

Così, per esempio, strutture fondamentali di massimo livello, così come sono state elaborate circa a partire dal 16° secolo in Italia come sottoprodotti indipendenti dell'arte tessile, si trovano ancora oggi – anche se copiati e variati, modificati e interpretati infinite volte – come elementi formali, come macro-ornamenti nella pubblicità o nella moda.

E vengono così usati, nel bazar della vanità e delle etichette, però abbelliscono senza dubbio il mondo della banalità quotidiana: sono geroglifici delle nostalgie.

e possibilità fondamentali di alternativa...

Non raramente gli elementi strutturali ingranditi infinitamente o fortemente alienati vengono a collisione con il complesso del loro materiale di partenza e sviluppano, posti in relazione tra loro, analogamente ai rapporti spazio-tempo, una relazione di tipo addirittura concettuale.

Macrotecnica come garante di una nuova ornamentistica, come catalizzatore per ricavare nuove qualità grafiche da idee formali, per tracciare nuovi contorni: icone della tecnica, dune mobili della fantasia.

al profilo vulnerabile del creativo.

Nella ricerca degli ornamenti del ricordo, dell'emigrazione nell'interiorità, incontriamo nei processi di trasformazione e nelle gallerie del nostro mondo di immagini e di motivi, l'almanacco di un arsenale inesauribile di disegni, le morbide geometrie delle nostre proprie immaginazioni: modelli di una deco–scatola di costruzioni, anatomie di paesaggi onirici.

Aus den detaillierten Dokumenten...

Wenn dekorative Zeichen und Motive in unserem Erinnerungsvermögen einen bleibenden Eindruck, gleichsam ein Muster prägen, und sich bei einer späteren, visuellen Wiederbegegnung (ähnlich dem Geruchsinn) wie auf Abruf erneut ein bestimmtes Empfinden, eine bereits vertraute Wahrnehumung einstellt, dann formen sich – Kindheitsträumen gleich – Ornamente der Erinnerung.

mit ihrem rätselhaften Hintergrundmaterial...

Unser Wortschatz und unser Sprachvermögen werden zweifellos nicht nur durch das soziale Umfeld oder durch die Erziehung gebildet, vielmehr entwickeln wir, unserem Charakter und unserem Temperament entsprechend, Vorlieben für bestimmte Sprach- und Satzkonstruktionen. Wir finden Gefallen am Klang und Rhythmus eigenwilliger Worte, die mehr versprechen als ihre bloße Bedeutung uns glauben schenken mag. Wir gewinnen Wortspielen und Kombinationen von Worten einen subtilen oder hintergründigen Reiz ab, weil sie unerwartete Assoziationen freisetzen, weil sie inspirativ, weil sie imaginativ wirken.

Unser Auge arbeitet nach einem ähnlichen Prinzip. Wir haben sie alle gespeichert oder sind zumindest bereit, sie in uns aufzunehmen, weil Farben und Formen Faszination auslösen und unsere Phantasie stimulieren: visuelle Images.

erschließt sich ein elementares Instrumentarium...

Die Möglichkeiten kreuzen sich. Einserseits lassen wir uns von Dingen des Alltags und von unserer näheren Umgebung beeinflussen, stellen spontan alle nur denkbaren Kombinationen in den Lichtkegel einer kreativen Sensibilität und erzielen dabei verheißungsvolle Resultate. Auf der anderen Seite ziehen wir Wissen und Erfahrungen von bereits erprobten Rezepten zu Rate, in der Hoffnung, durch spezielle Montagetechniken oder raffinierte Beleuchtungsmethoden ein anderes Licht, eine extreme Variante, die Algebra eine Hyperkreativität zu entdecken.

Doch wenn sich letzlich herausstellt, daß wir weniger eine neue Syntax entwickelt als vielmehr aus Versatzstücken, Ideenfragmenten und Ornamentsplittern einen neuen Kontext arrangiert haben, drängt sich die Frage auf, worauf wir denn ständing und stetig zurückgreifen: auf dekorative Vorbilder.

versehen mit Chiffren geheimster Gleichungen...

Die Zeichen- und Bildersprache der modernen Gebrauchsgrafik wie auch die der internationalen "High Fashion" zeigt in endlosen Retrospektiven Reihen von ständig wiederkehrenden Mustern und Motiven, die Teil einer dekorativen Grammatik zu sein scheinen, auf die sich, kulturgeschichtlich bedingt, wohl nicht verzichten läßt.

So finden sich zum Beispiel Grundstrukturen von Spitzen, wie sie sich etwa seit dem 16. Jahrhundert in Italien als selbständige Nebenprodukte der Textilkunst entwickelten, noch heute, wenn auch unendlich oft kopiert und variiert, modifiziert und interpretiert, als Formelemente, als Makro-Ornamente in der Werbung oder in der Mode wieder.

Folglich werden sie gebraucht, auf dem Bazaar der Eitelkeiten und Etiketten, verschönern sie doch ohne Zweifel die Welt des täglichen Allerlei: Hieroglyphen der Sehnsüchte.

und fundamentalen Möglichkeiten zur Alternative...

Nicht selten kollidieren unendlich vergrößerte oder stark verfremdete Strukturelemente mit der Gesamtheit ihres Ausgangsmaterials und entwickeln, miteinander in Beziehung gebracht, ähnlich den Raum-Zeit-Verhältnissen, eine geradezu konzeptuelle Relation.

Makrotechnik als Garant einer neuen Ornamentik, als Katalysator, um festen Formvorstellungen neue grafische Qualitäten abzugewinnen, um neue Konturen zu ziehen: Ikonen der Technik, Wanderdünen der Phantasie.

dem Wundprofil der Kreativen.

Auf der Suche nach den Ornamenten der Erinnerung, der Emigration ins Innere, begegnen wir in den Wandelgängen und Galerien unserer Bilder- und Motivwelt, dem Almanach eines unerschöpflichen Design-Arsenals, den weichen Geometrien unserer eigenen Imaginationen: Modelle eines Deco-Baukastens, Anatomien von Traumlandschaften.

De los documentos detallados...

Si dibujos decorativos y motivos dejan en nuestra memoria una impresión persistente y al mismo tiempo un modelo y si durante un encuentro visual sucesivo (análogamente a lo que sucede con el olfato) se establece, como ante una llamada, otra vez una nueva sensación, una percepción familiar, entonces se forman así como sucede en los sueños de la infancia-adornos del recuerdo.

con su material enigmático de fondo...

Nuestro patrimonio y nuestra capacidad linguística no se forman indudablemente solo por el ambiente social o por la educación, sino que nosotros desarrollamos, de acuerdo con nuestro carácter y nuestro temperamento, una preferencia por determinadas estructuras linguísticas y por determinado modo de frasear. Encontramos placer en el sonido o en el ritmo de palabras bizarras que son más prometentes de lo que pueda hacernos creer su simple significado: obtenemos de ciertos juegos de palabras y combinaciones de palabras un estímulo sutil o recóndito dado que los mismos liberan asociaciones inesperadas, actúan como inspiración, actúan como imaginación.

Nuestro ojo trabaja de acuerdo con un principio análogo. Hemos memorizado todos estos elementos o estamos al menos listos para recibirlos dentro nuestro, ya que los colores y las formas producen encanto y estimulan nuestra fantasía: imágenes visuales.

se abre un instrumental elemental...

Las posibilidades se entrecruzan. Por un lado nos dejamos influenciar por cosas obtenidas del ritmo cotidiano y del ambiente que nos circunda, ponemos espontáneamente todas las posibles combinaciones en el cono de luz de una sensibilidad creativa, obteniendo en tal forma, resultados plenos de promesas. Por otra parte, recurrimos al conocimiento y a las experiencias ya probadas, con la esperanza de descubrir, mediante técnicas especiales de montaje o métodos refinados de illuminación, otra luz, una variante extrema, el álgebra de una hiperactividad.

Sin embargo, cuando finalmente se descubre que hemos desarrollado no tanto una nueva sintaxis sino que hemos elaborado un nuevo contexto partiendo de elementos escénicos móviles, fragmentos de ideas y porciones ornamentales, surge el interrogante de dónde recurrimos permanente y constantemente: a los ejemplos decorativos.

provisto con cifras de ecuaciones secretas...

El lenguaje de los signos y de las imágenes de la moderna gráfica usual, como también el de la "high fashion" internacional, muestra en retrospectiva, series interminables de modelos y motivos siempre recurrentes que parecen formar parte de una gramática decorativa a la cual justamente no se puede renunciar por motivos conectados con la historia de la cultura. De esta forma, por ejemplo, estructuras fundamentales de máximo nivel, tal como han sido elaboradas más o menos a partir del siglo XVI en Italia como subproductos independientes del arte textil, se encuentran aún hoy-aunque copiadas y variadas, modificadas e interpretadas infinitas veces-como elementos formales, como macro-ornamentos en la publicidad o en la moda. Y así son usadas, en el bazar de la vanidad y de las etiquetas, embelleciendo sin duda el mundo de la banalidad cotidiana: son jeroglíficos de la nostalgia.

y posibilidades fundamentales de alternativas...

No es extraño que los elementos estructurales aumentados infinitamente o muy alienados choquen con la totalidad del material de partida y desarrollen, relacionados entre sí, análogamente con las relaciones espacio-tiempo, una correspondencia de tipo justamente conceptual.
Macrotécnica como garantía de una nueva ornamentística, como catalizador para obtener nuevas cualidades gráficas de ideas formales, para trazar nuevos contornos: ícono de la técnica, dunas movedizas de la fantasía.

al perfil vulnerario del creador.

En la búsqueda de los ornamentos de recuerdo, de la emigración en la interioridad, encontramos en los procesos de transformación y en los túneles de nuestro mundo de imágenes y motivos, el almanaque de un arsenal inagotable de diseños, las mórbidas geometrías de nuestras propias imaginaciones: modelos de un juego de armar, anatomías de paisajes oníricos.

Des documents détaillés...

Si les dessins décoratifs et les motifs laissent, dans notre mémoire, une impression persistante en même temps qu'un modèle et si, au cours d'une rencontre visuelle ultérieure (de façon analogue à ce qui a lieu pour l'odorat), il se détermine de nouveau, comme par l'effet d'un rappel, une sensation nouvelle, une perception familière, alors il se forme – ainsi que cela se produit pour les rêves de notre enfance – des enjolivements du souvenir.

avec leur matériel énigmatique d'arrière–plan...

Notre patrimoine et notre capacité linguistiques ne sont certainement pas formés uniquement par le milieu social ou par l'éducation, mais nous élaborons, selon notre caractère et notre tempérament, une préférence à l'égard de structures linguistiques et de tournures déterminées. Nous éprouvons du plaisir au son et au rythme de paroles bizzares qui sont plus prometteuses que ce que pourrait nous faire croire leur signification pure et simple: nous tirons de certains jeux de mots, de certaines combinaisons de mots, une impulsion subtile ou secrète du fait qu'ils dégagent des associations inattendues, qu'ils agissent comme une inspiration, qu'ils opèrent en tant qu'imagination.
Notre oeil travaille suivant un principe analogue.
Nous avons mémorisé tous ces éléments et nous sommes prêts, pour le moins, à les accueillir en nous, car les couleurs et les formes dégagent du charme et stimulent notre fantaisie: images visuelles.

s'ouvre un attirail élémentaire...

Les possibilités s'entrecroisent. D'une part, nous nous laissons influencer par des choses tirées des rythmes quotidiens et du milieu qui nous entoure, nous plaçons spontanément toutes les combinaisons possibles dans le cône de lumière d'une sensibilité créatrice et nous réalisons ainsi des résultats riches de promesses. D'autre part, nous avons recours au savoir et aux expériences de recettes déjà éprouvées, dans l'espoir de découvrir, grâce à des techniques spéciales de montage ou à des méthodes raffinées d'éclairage, une autre lumière, une variante extrême, l'algèbre d'une hyper–créativité. Cependant, lorsqu'il s'avère enfin qu'au lieu d'avoir forgé véritablement une nouvelle syntaxe, nous avons plutôt élaboré un nouveau contexte à partir d'éléments scéniques mobiles, de fragments d'idées et d'éclats de décors, la question se pose de savoir où nous puisons de façon permanente et constante: dans des exemples décoratifs.

pourvu de chiffres d'équations secrètes...

Le langage des signes et des images de l'art graphique courant, comme aussi de la "high fashion" internationale montre, en rétrospective, d'interminables séries de modèles et de motifs, toujours récurents et qui semblent faire partie d'une grammaire décorative à laquelle justement on ne peut renoncer pour des raisons liées à l'histoire de la culture.

C'est ainsi, par exemple, que des structures fondamentales de très haut niveau, telles qu'elles ont été élaborées à dater, à peu près, du XVIe siècle, en Italie, se retrouvent, aujourd'hui encore – bien que copiées et variées, modifiées et interprétées un nombre infini de fois – en tant qu'éléments de forme, comme macro–ornements, dans la publicité et dans la mode.

Et c'est ainsi qu'elles sont utilisées dans le bazar de la vanité et des étiquettes; toutefois, elles embellisent, sans aucun doute, le monde de la banalité quotidienne: ce sont les hiéroglyphes des nostalgies.

et de possibilités fondamentales d'une solution de rechange...

Il n'est pas rare que les éléments structurels, infiniment agrandis ou fortement aliénés, entrent en collision avec l'ensemble de leur matériel de départ et donnent lieu, lorsqu'ils sont mis en relation entre eux – de façon analogue aux rapports espace-temps – à une relation de type même conceptuel.

Macrotechnique en tant que garante de l'art de la décoration, en tant que catalyseur pour pouvoir tirer de nouvelles qualités graphiques des idées de la forme, pour tracer de nouveaux contours: icônes de la technique, dunes mobiles de l'imagination.

par rapport à l'image vulnéraire de l'esprit créateur.

Dans la recherche des ornements du souvenir, de l'émigration de l'antériorité, nous rencontrons, dans les processus de transformation et dans les galeries de notre monde d'images et de motifs, l'almanach d'un arsenal inépuisable de dessins, les formes géométriques souples de nos propres imaginations: modèles d'un kit d'éléments décoratifs composables, anatomies de paysages oniriques.

Most of the following plates in polychrome and monochrome were created and developed in the studio & laboratory of Edition Belvedere in Rome, Italy under the general direction of Wolfgang Hageney.

A part of the color motifs (20 plates) derives from the original Art Deco Portfolio Edition "La Décoration Moderne Dans Le Textile" by Gaston Charlet, published by Ch. Massin & Cie. in Paris around 1930. These plates were printed and colored in the pochoir technique.

The cover of this volume was created and developed in the studio & laboratory of Edition Belvedere. Design by Diana Lelli.

21

23

24

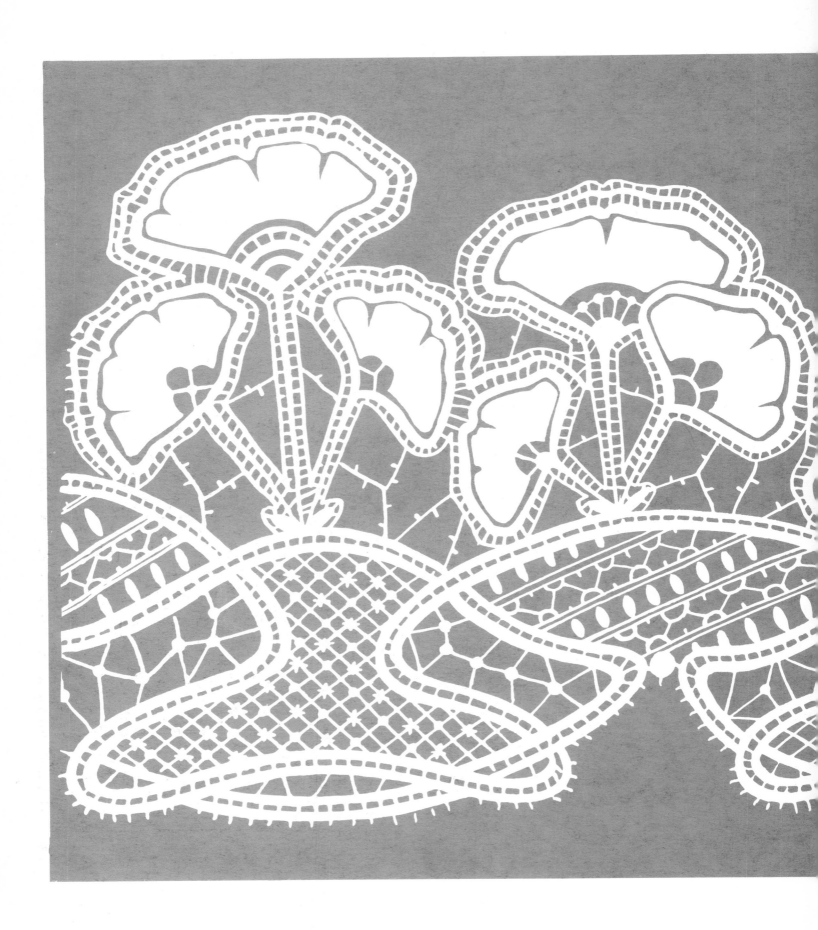

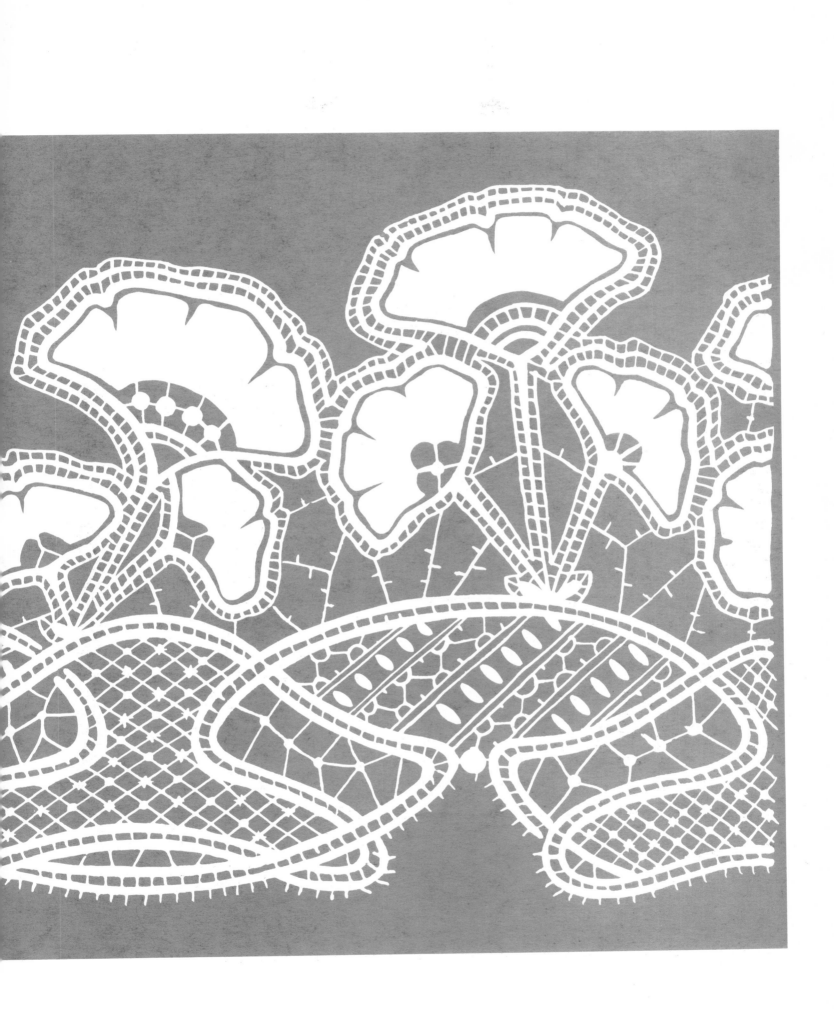

28

29

34

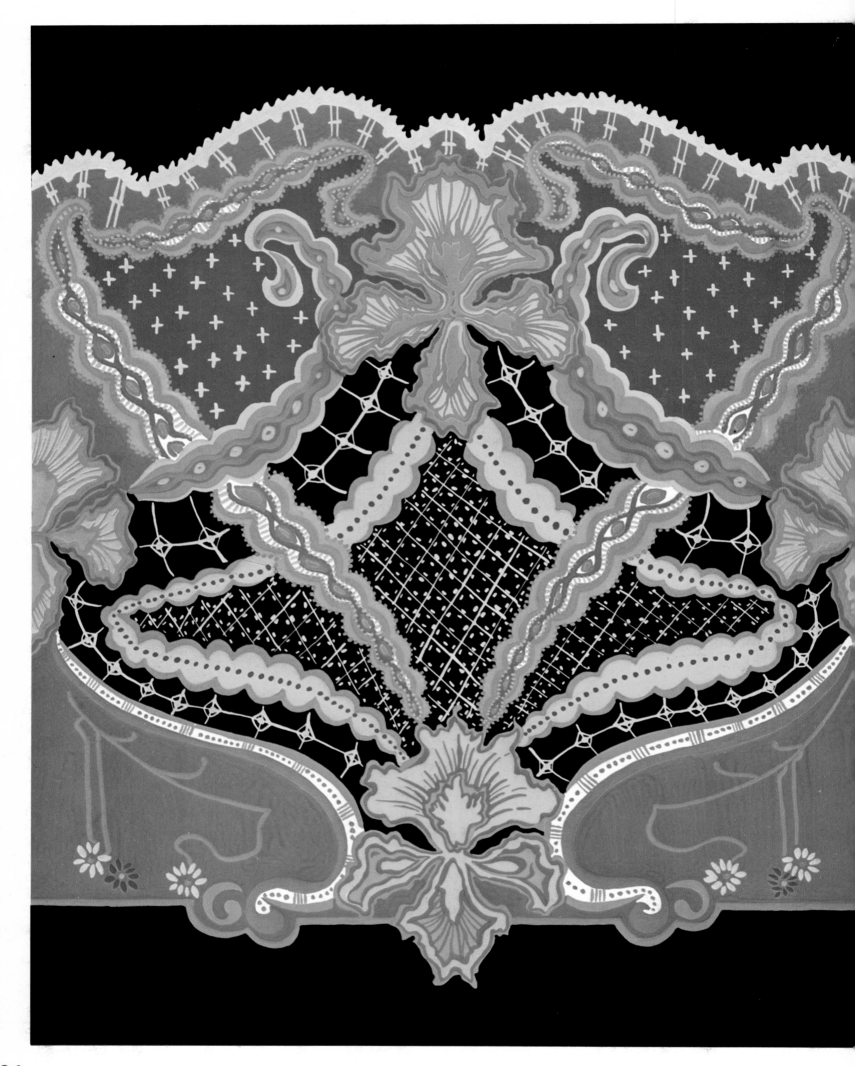

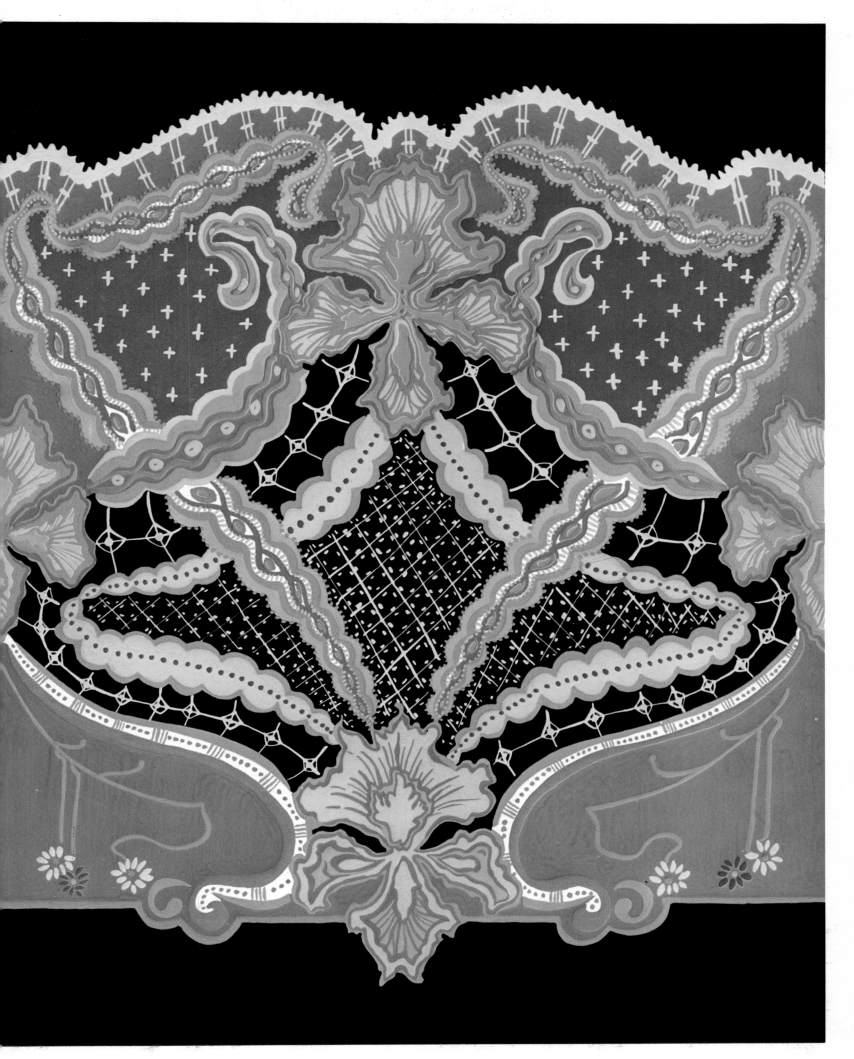

37

41

45

47

48

49

52

54

63

64

73

89

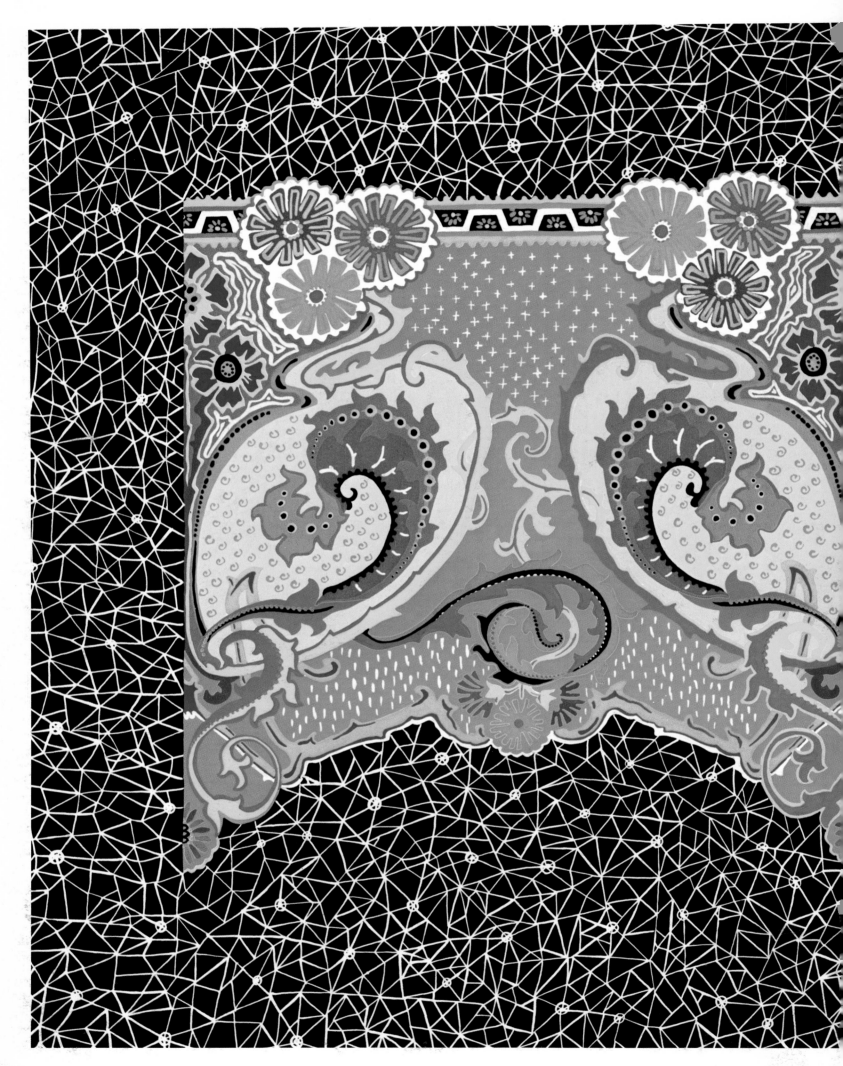

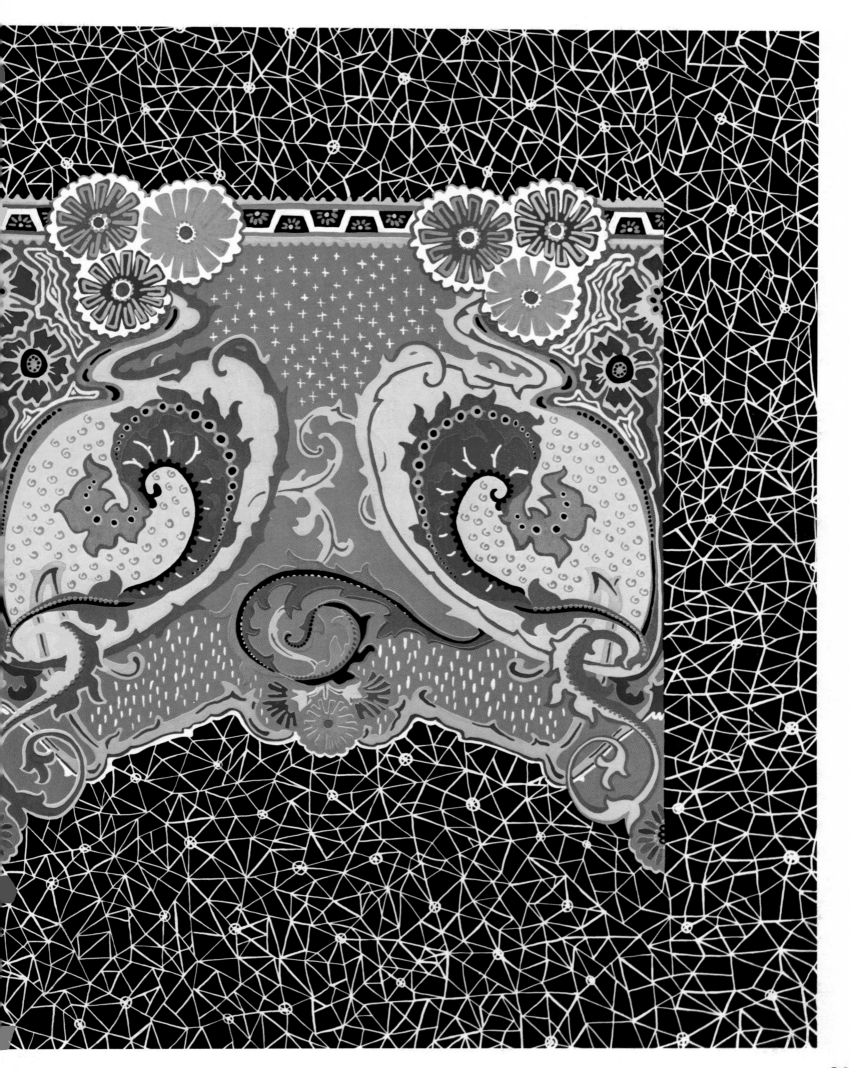

93

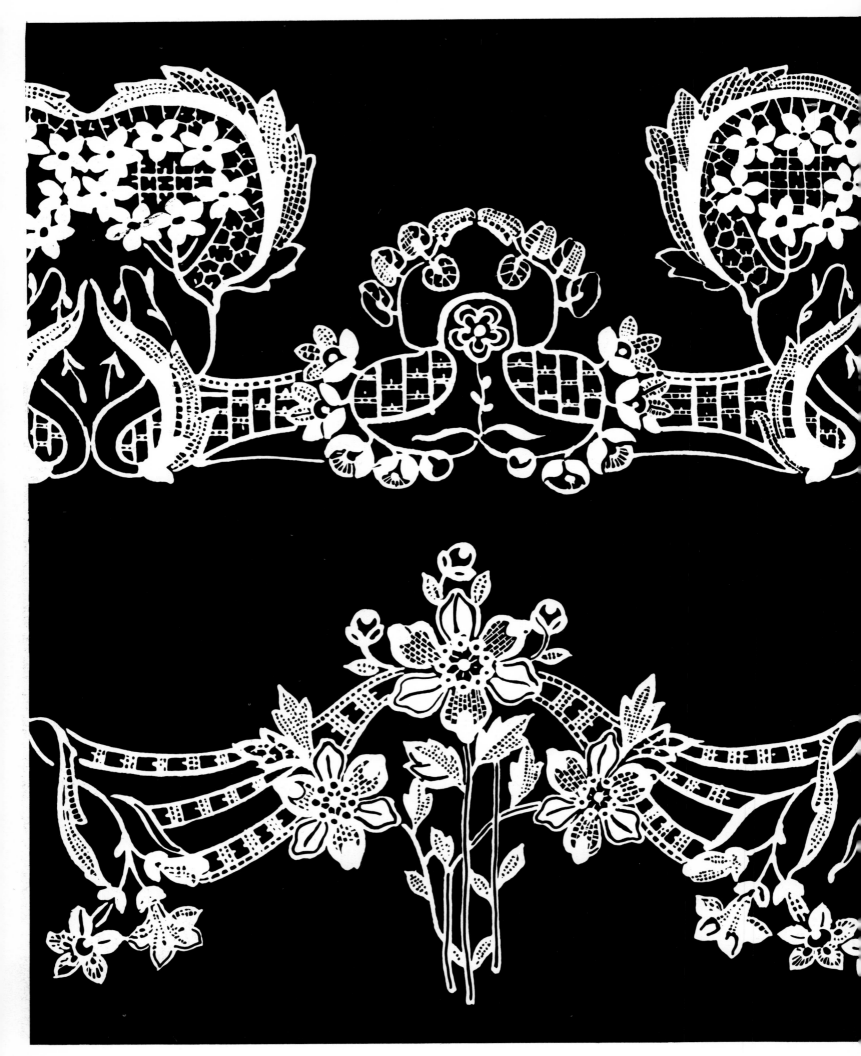

94

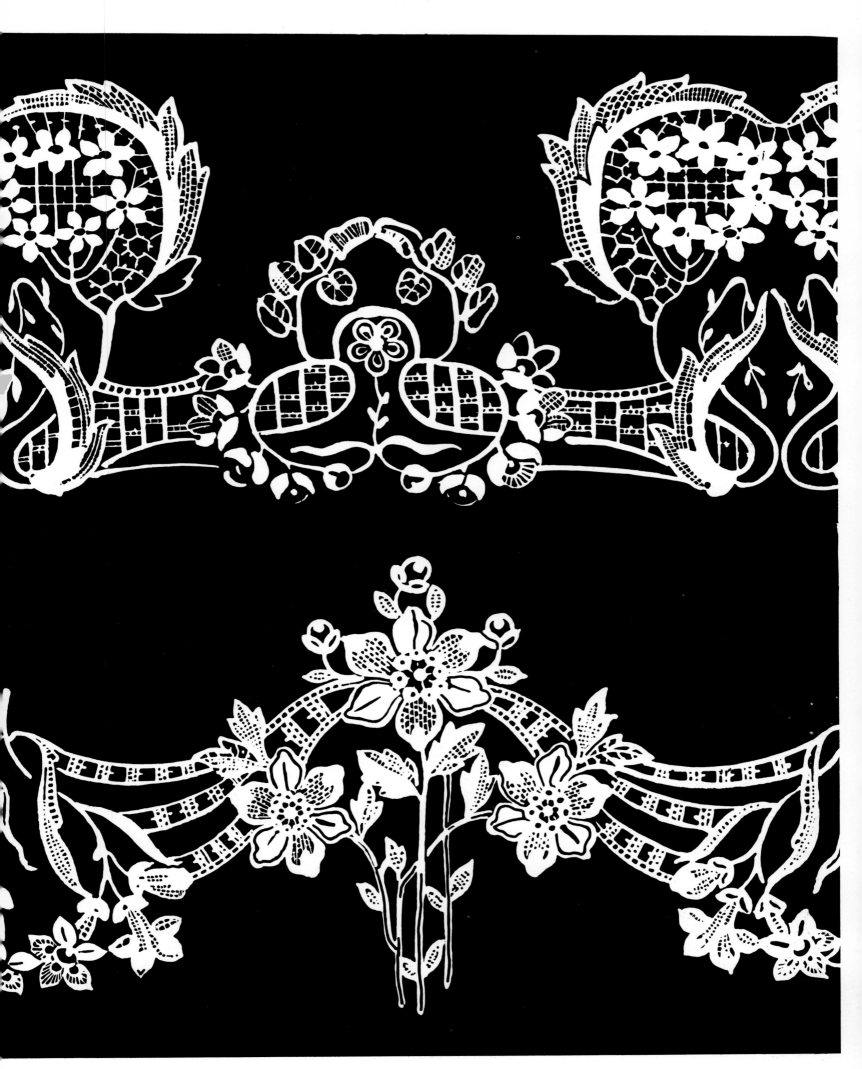

102

103

108

109

112

114

115

120

123

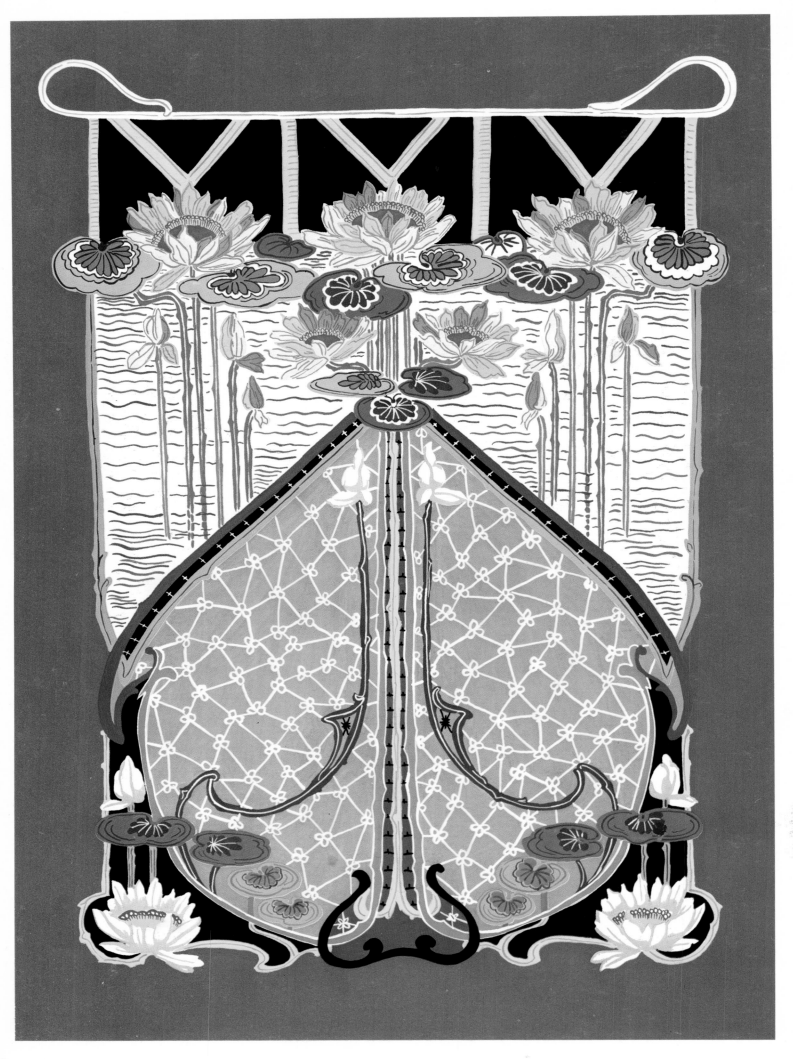

124

128

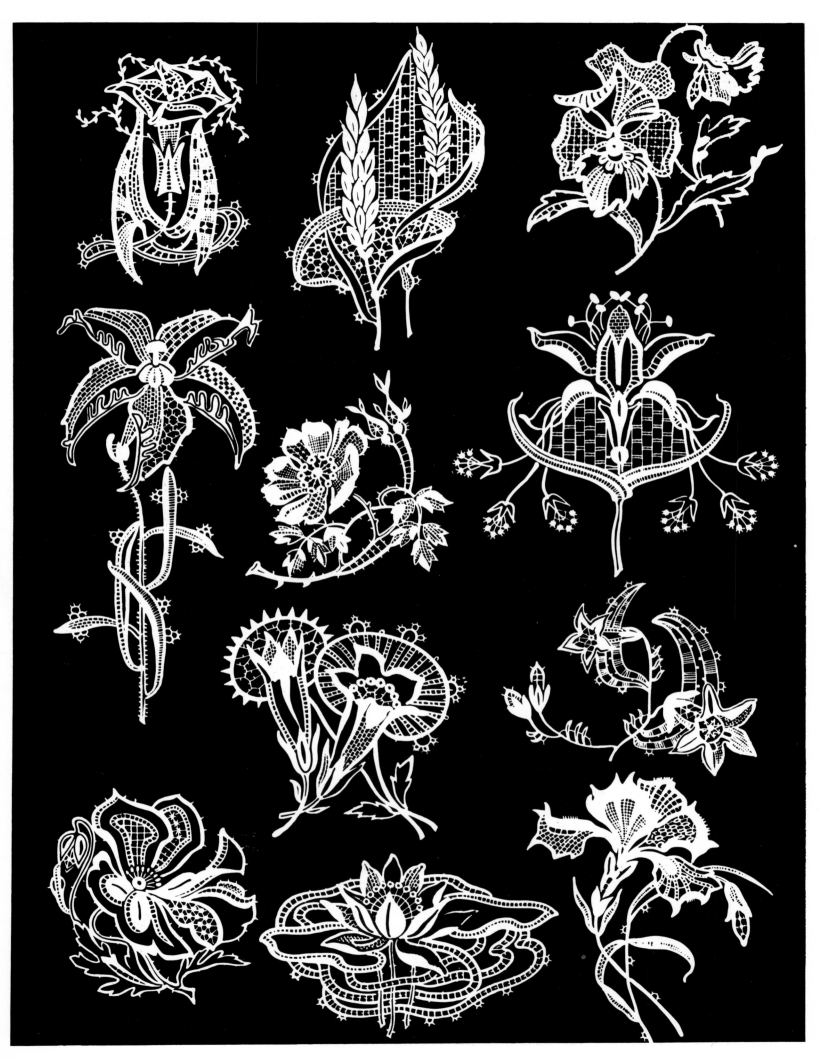

130

138

139

141

144

146

148

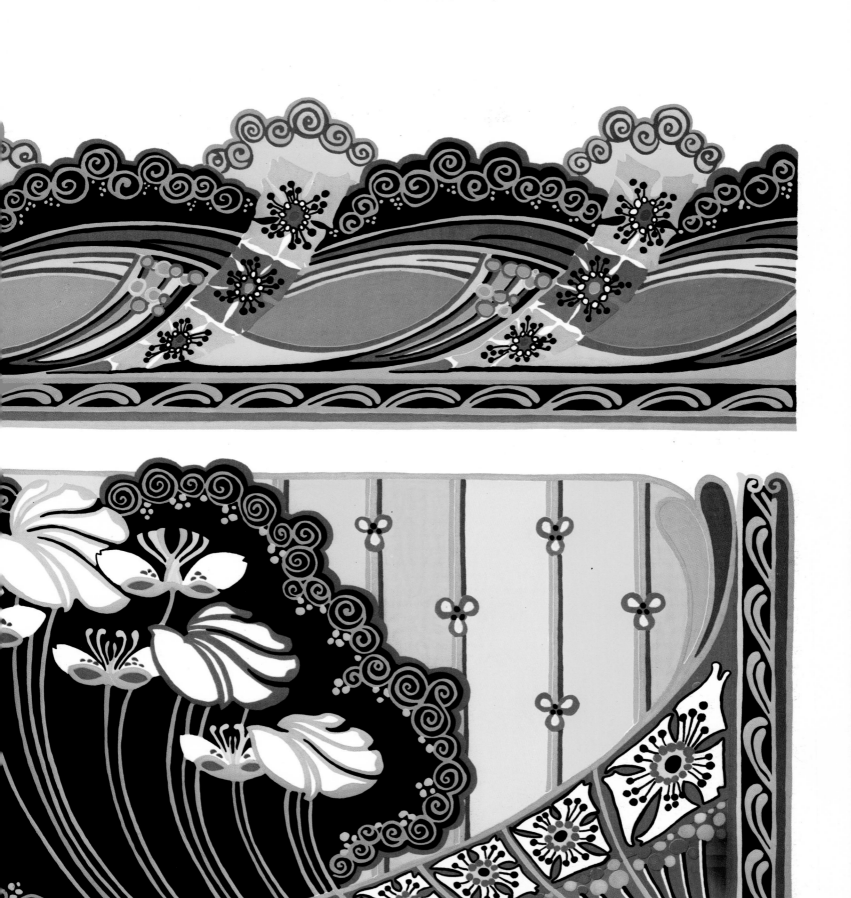

149

150

153

157

163

167

171

172

180

181

190

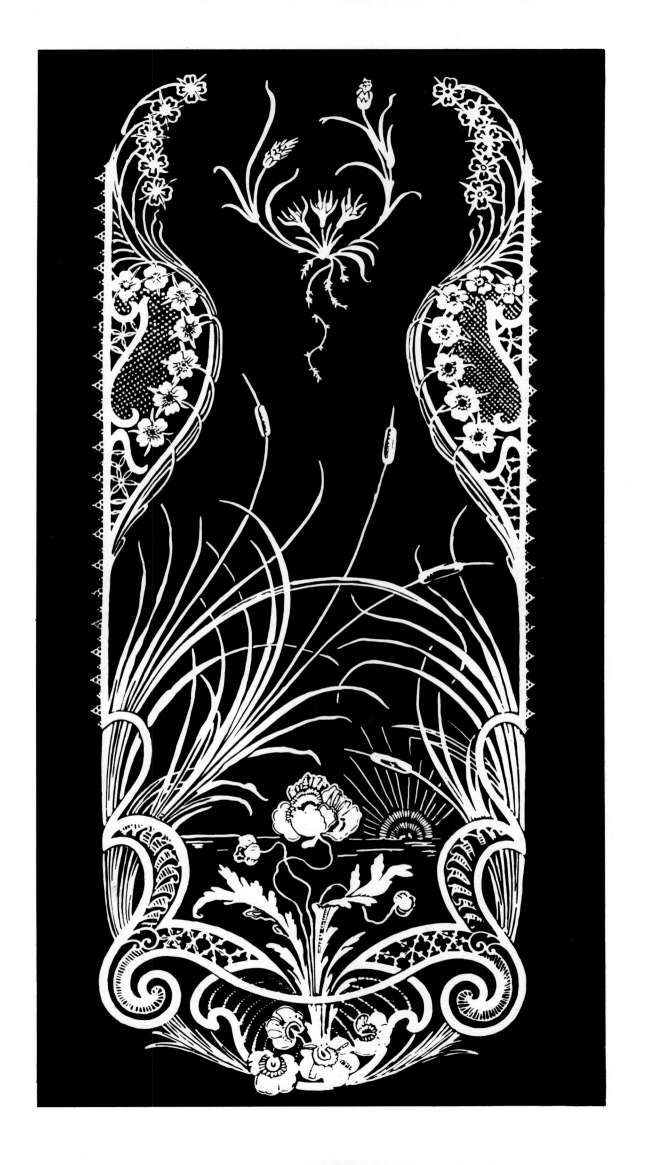

191

194

195

a name......a programm.....

BELVEDERE
BOOKS FOR FASHION, DECORATION, ARCHITECTURE, PHOTOGRAPHY & GRAPHIC DESIGN

Natural Flowers & H

erbs

FLOWER COMPOSITION is based upon dress fabrics. 100 different floral motifs with 400 suggested exemplary variations are printed on both sides of 150 plates. The imagination is stimulated by the variations, first of all in the opposition of equal sized designs in positive-negative effect, then the reverse side variation. Other examples are the reduction of the same design or the blow-up of one pattern section. In the play between shade and contrast, positive and negative, size and choice of side, the structure and its individual elements produce a varied effect so that by direct comparison, time and effort consuming preparation can be saved. In this way coordination and repeat, composition and size become more easily recognizable, allowances for the different seasons and markets can be made more quickly. The choice of fabric can be readily imagined. Technical printing problems can be examined at the preliminary stages of production.

FLOWER COMPOSITION does not present its flower motifs as copies of nature, neither is it concerned with realistic structure or form. Instead, it transforms and portrays flowers in optical-graphical movement creating a composition which is specially suited to fashion fabrics.

300 pages, 400 motifs, monochrome, black/white, book box, bound in cotton canvas, single plates: 31 x 43 cm.

BELVEDERE HARDCOVER

EXAMPLES OF CHINESE ORNAMENT

100 Plates in colour selected from objects in the South Kensington Museum and other collectors

by

OWEN JONES

Examples of Chinese Ornament was first published in London 1867. Today the work is one of the most sought-after antiquarian books of the Victorian Era and art collectors consider it to be a bibliophil's rarity. This Reprint is based on an original 1867 draft.

Owen Jones, as an English architect, designer and writer was particular inspired by Islamic art. In his capacity as superintendent of works for The Great London Exhibition 1851, he created a new style of design for The Crystal Palace at Sydenham. In 1856 he first published his major work with the title *Grammar of Ornament*, the first comprehensive illustrated book about the ornaments of different peoples, cultural circles and epochs.

« We have long been familiar with the power of the Chinese to balance colours, but we were not so well acquainted with their power of treating purely ornamental or conventional forms...

...The position of the larger flowers was fixed in the position most suited to develope the peculiar form of the vase, and the whole surface was set out by these flowers into symmetrical proportional areas; here law and order were abandoned, and the instinct and caprice of the artist came into play, in uniting all these fixed centres by a flowing line. This flowing line then dividing the different triangular spaces irregularly, masses of intermediate size, either as flowers or large leaves, were put in, springing from the continuous line; these secondary masses also balance triangularly, but in a less rigid manner than with the larger flowers: the process is continued by the introduction within the intermediate spaces of still smaller forms, buds, or stalks, till the whole is filled up, and repose is obtained by evenness of tint. This method of composition is followed in all the Oriental styles of ornament: what is peculiar to the Chinese, especially in their large enamelled objects, is the large relative size of the principal flowers which mark the triangulation of the areas; and it will be seen throughout the plates how cleverly this apparent disproportion of the principal points of the composition is got over by the detail on the surface of the flower, so that the desirable evenness of tint is preserved...

...The scheme of colouring of the Chinese is peculiarly their own. They deal principally with broken colours: pale blue, pale green, and pale pink for the masses; dark pink, dark green, purple, and yellow and white, in much smaller quantities. There is nothing crude or harsh in any of their compositions; the eye is perfectly satisfied with the balance and arrangement of both form and colour... »

Preface to *Examples of Chinese Ornament*

ISBN 88-7070-003-8

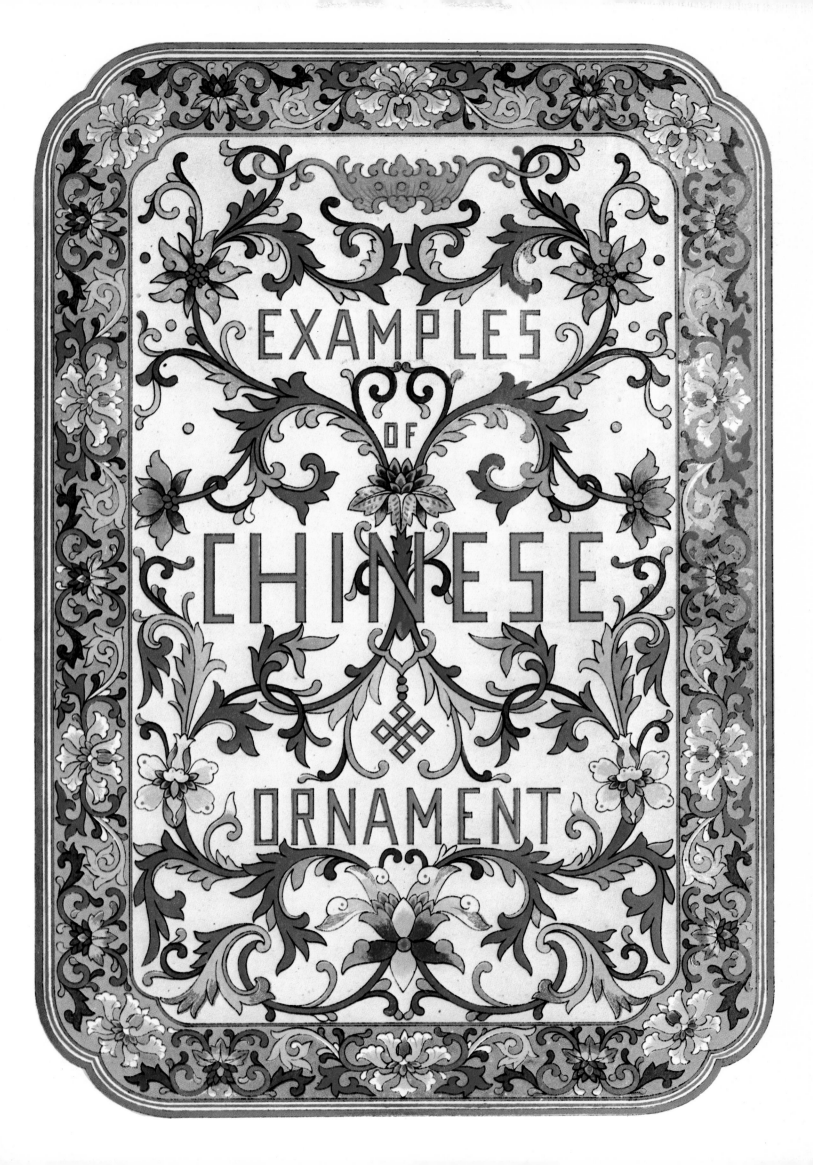

EXAMPLES
OF
CHINESE
ORNAMENT

BELVEDERE BOOK BOXES

FLOWER COMPOSITION

Based upon dress fabrics of 1940 - 100 different floral motifs with 400 suggested exemplary variations are printed on both sides of 150 single plates, with positive-negative-effects, reductions and blow-ups.

Flower Composition does not present its flower motifs as copies of nature, neither is it concerned with realistic structure or form. Instead, it transforms and portrays flowers in optical-graphical movement creating a composition which is specially suited to fashion fabrics.

300 pages, 400 motifs, monochrome - black/white
book box, bound in cotton canvas - black.
single plates: 31 x 43 cm,

NATURAL FLOWER & HERBS

68 suggested variations presenting an immense number of different floral motifs based upon mountain flowers and herbs. The flower plates are painted with an extremely high quality more than 150 years ago by a Japanese artist with a particular handwriting.

The book is reproduced in a monochrome technique. Each composition is printed on a single plate (horizontal 31 x 43 cm). In addition the book contains 8 plates in a polychrome version (full color).

The edition includes a rich album which names all the flowers and herbs by reduced illustrations.

76 plates, 8 full-page color plates, incl. album,
single plates: 31 x 43 cm,
book box, bound in cotton canvas - blue.

FLORAL ART

60 plates of floral designs of 1932, when the book was published for the first time. Floral Art - Decoration and Design certainly is a work of the kind that all should welcome, whether they are primarily interested in the design of flowers as such or as integral elements of decoration.

The illustrations are as practical as they are varied and abundant and finely reproduced in colorphoto system. Size of each reproduction: 16 x 23 cm.

60 plates, all in color, **Limited Edition,**
single plates: 31 x 43 cm, book box, bound in cotton canvas - dark red.

BELVEDERE BOOK BOXES

FLOWER & ORNAMENT

This book is influenced by the "Jugenstil". All motifs were originated between 1910-1920. On 72 plates are presented more than 450 floral & ornamental motifs, printed in a polychrome version - all in full color. There are mainly ideas from or for wallpaper, mural painting, interior design and carpets, mostly in combination: graphic or ornamental elements composed with floral motifs.

72 plates, 450 motifs, all in color, incl. album,
single plates: 31 x 43 cm,
book box, bound in cotton canvas - red.

BLUMEN

72 floral plates (printed in polychrome & monochrome) with many single motifs. The volume is divided into three sections - I. 24 floral plates with 60 different motifs, originated around 1915, all in color. II. 24 floral designs, possible adaptions/interpretations from the originals, also all in color. III. 24 basic compositions with elements from the designs of part II, in monochrome - black and white.
The edition includes an album which indicates all flowers' names are shown in the book.

72 plates, polychrome & monochrome, incl. album, single plates: 31 x 43 cm, book box, bound in cotton canvas - light brown.

THE PLANTS OF 1917

125 floral reproductions - all in full color - showing garden plants of the four seasons. In the year 1917, based on European flowers, the plates were painted in Japanese handwriting in watercolor technique with an extremely high quality. The motifs are divided in 50 plates of the spring season, 50 plates of the summer season and 25 plates with both - autumn and winter flowers.
The edition indicates in the front page all flowers names which are shown in the book.

66 plates, 125 colorphoto reproductions, all in color,
single plates: 34 x 48 cm,
book box, bound in cotton canvas - green.
Limited Edition.

BEAUTIES OF NATURE

The volume shows 48 single plates with beautiful flower illustrations, painted in 1896. The reproduction is made in colorphoto system. Each volume is handmade. The book is represented in a box and includes an album which indicates all flowers name are shown in the book. Beauties of Nature is an individual an limited edition.

48 plates, all in color, incl. album,
Limited Edition, *single plates: 31 x 43 cm, book box, bound in cotton canvas - grey.*

BELVEDERE BOOK BOXES

The book boxes of the Edition Belvedere offer professional material for artists, stylists and designers in the field of textile and fashion. The above mentioned boxes are strictly limited editions and they are available only directly from the publisher. For further information, conditions and prices write to:
EDITION BELVEDERE CO. LTD., 00196 ROME/ITALY, PIAZZALE FLAMINIO 19, TEL. (06) 360.44.88/360.29.60.

All volumes are representing single plates, mostly 31 x 43 cm, on heavy paper, and they are collect in a box, bound in cotton canvas.

BELVEDERE BOOK BOXES

GRAPHICOLOR
300 GRAPHICAL MOTIFS WITH FANTASY ALL IN COLOR

BELVEDERE

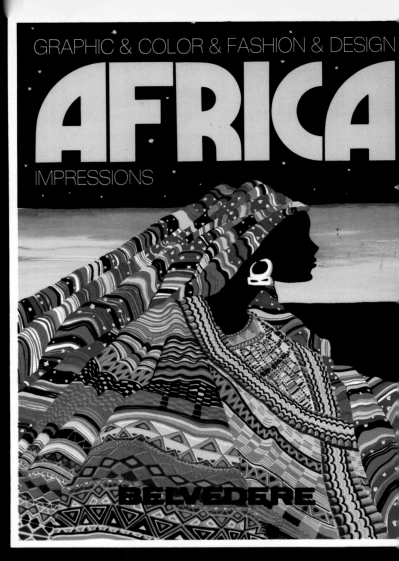

GRAPHIC & COLOR & FASHION & DESIGN

AFRICA
IMPRESSIONS

BELVEDERE

ARCHI
»TEXTURE«

BELVEDERE

Bouquets

BELVEDERE

DECOR

BELVEDERE

Oriental flowers

BELVEDERE

FLORAL
DREAM

BELVEDERE

MEMORY
LACE DESIGNS · A VERSION OF TEXTILE DECORATION
FROM 1920-1930

BELVEDERE

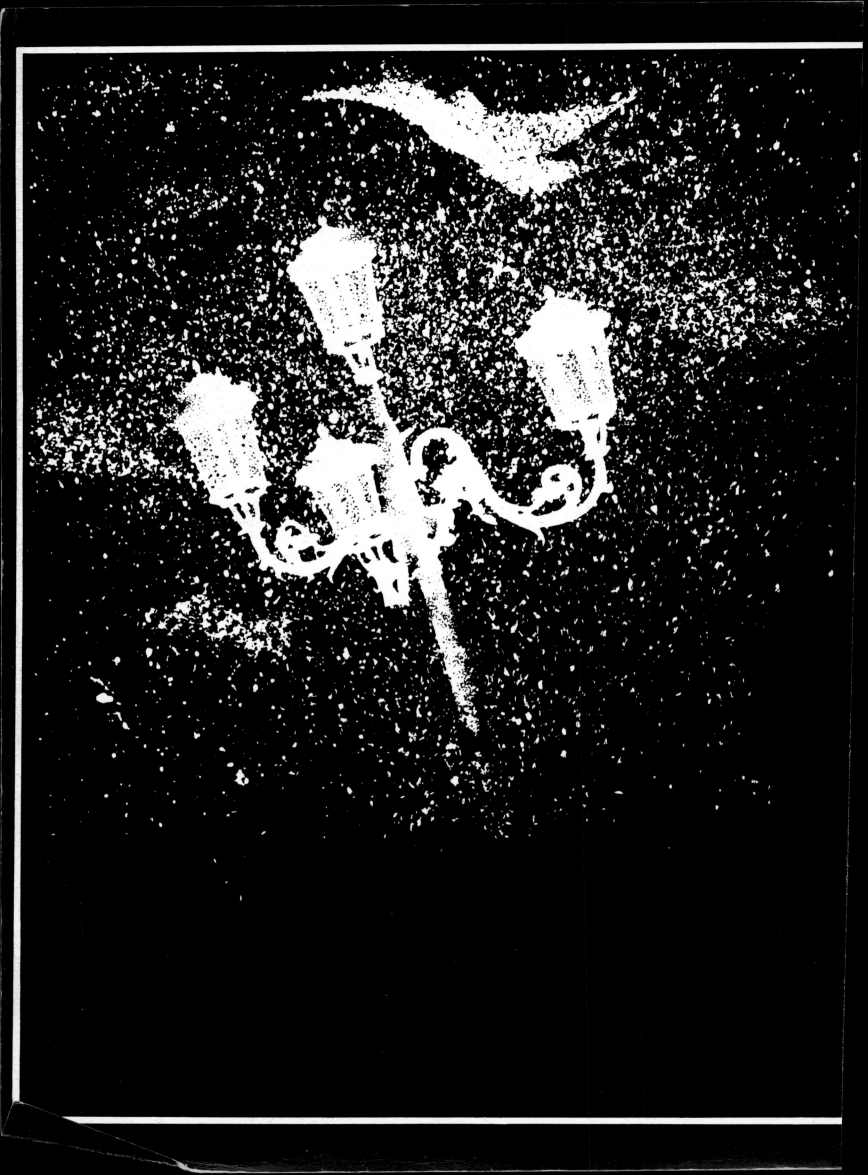

MEMORY

BELVEDERE

BELVEDERE-PAPERBACKS
VOLUME 9

COSTUMES
FRENCH FEMALE 1037-1870

BELVEDERE

At the time of the Crusades, a cultural exchange took place between the peoples of the East and West. One of its consequences was without doubt a new development of the way in which people in Europe dressed. This was not just a question of taste or a new feeling for colors, style and cutting, but essentially the embodiment of new-won knowledge of hitherto unknown fabrics and materials, patterns and ornaments, that laid the foundations for the richness and elegance of costume. The present book offers the reader a wealth of information which testifies to the imaginativeness and refinement of ideas displayed in the history of costume and shows to what an extent the periods under review still continue to influence styles in fashion trends today.

ISBN 88-7070-009-7

What
style of art is still
the most imaginative
today?